INDOOR/ OUTDOOR

Kenny Finkle

BROADWAY PLAY PUBLISHING INC
224 E 62nd St, NY NY 10065-8201
212 772-8334 fax: 212 772-8358
BroadwayPlayPubl.com

1st printing: Feb 2007; this printing: April 2011
I S B N: 978-0-88145-330-0

Book design: Marie Donovan
Word processing: Microsoft Word
Typographic controls: Ventura Publisher
Typeface: Palatino
Printed and bound in the U S A

ABOUT THE AUTHOR

Kenny Finkle's play INDOOR/OUTDOOR recently received its off-Broadway premiere at the DR2 in Union Square. The play has also been produced at Trinity Repertory, Virginia Stage Company Summer Play Festival, the Colony Theater and the Hangar Theater. Other plays include: BRIDEZILLA STRIKES BACK (co-written with Cynthia Silver, N Y Fringe Festival, 2005), TRANSATLANTICA (Flea Theatre, 2002), and JOSH KEENAN COMES OUT TO THE WORLD (Philadelphia Gay and Lesbian Theater Festival and Hangar Theater School Tour, 2003/4). He is a recipient of a N Y F A fellowship, was awarded University of Illinois' Inner Voices prize and has received commissions from the Hangar Theater in Ithaca, NY and Ford's Theater in Washington, DC. Kenny is a graduate of Columbia University's M F A Playwriting program and a member of the Dramatists Guild.

INDOOR/OUTDOOR was originally produced by the Hangar Theater (Artistic Director, Kevin Moriarty; Executive Director, Lisa Bushlow) in Ithaca, NY, opening on 21 July 2004. The cast and creative contributors were:

SAMANTHA . . . . Jenny Maguire
SHUMAN . . . . Michael Bakkensen
MATILDA . . . . .Brandy Zarle
OSCAR . . . . Tommy Schrider

Director . . . . .Kevin Moriarty
Set design . . . . .Beowolf Boritt
Costume design . . . . Greg Robbins
Sound design . . . . Ryan Rummery
Lighting design . . . . .Jeff Croiter
Stage manager . . . . Monika Tandon
Casting . . . . .Stephanie Klapper

INDOOR/OUTDOOR was produced Off Broadway*
at the D R 2 Theater in New York, NY by Daryl Roth,
Margo Lion, Hal Luftig in association with Lily Hung.
It opened on 22 February 2006 with the following cast
and creative contributors:

SAMANTHA .... Emily Cass McDonnell
SHUMAN......................... Brian Hutchison
MATILDA .... Keira Naughton
OSCAR .... Mario Campanaro

Director ....Daniel Goldstein
Set Design ....David Korins
Costume Design .... Michael Krass
Sound Design ...Walter Trarbach & Tony Smolenski IV
Lighting Design .... Ben Stanton
Stage Manager ....Brian Maschka
Casting .... Stephanie Klapper

*originally produced in N Y C at the Summer Play Festival
July 2005*

CHARACTERS & SETTING

SAMANTHA, *a cat*

SHUMAN, *the man who brings her home*

MATILDA, *receptionist at the vet and a burgeoning Cat Therapist (This actor should play* MOM.*)*

OSCAR, *another cat. (This actor plays all other characters.)*

The majority of the action takes place in and around SHUMAN'*s house.*

AUTHOR'S NOTE

SAMANTHA, MOM *and* OSCAR *should not be played with any physical indication that they are cats. I like to think of the play and the characters as being written in primary colors. There is very little subtext. Characters say what they feel or are unable to say what they feel but are completely transparent in it. They are earnest, they are pure, they do not comment on the action or themselves.*

SPECIAL THANKS

Kevin Moriarty, Beth Whitaker, and Mark Subias

DEDICATION

For Matthew, Beverly, and of course the real Samantha.

ACT ONE

(*Lights up on* SAMANTHA *sitting by herself on the edge of the stage.*)

SAMANTHA: (*To audience*) Hi. My name's Samantha and these are my memoirs.

(*Just then* SHUMAN *appears on stage, looking for* SAMANTHA.)

SHUMAN: Samantha? SAMANTHA?? (He wanders off.)

SAMANTHA: That's Shuman. I live with him. He's looking for me right now. We'll get to him in a minute. First though, you need to know me. O K. From the beginning. This is how I was born.

(MOM *appears and stands with her legs wide open. She grunts. And grunts again. And then screams. On the scream* SAMANTHA *slides in between her legs with her eyes closed. She screams too. Then looks around*)

SAMANTHA: Wow! I'm alive! Finally! Oh wow, I'm tired. Hi, you must be my Mom. I'd recognize you anywhere.

MOM: Listen darling, I'd love to chat right now but I've got twenty more of you coming.

(MOM *starts to grunt again.* SAMANTHA *moves out of the way and* MOM *leaves.*)

SAMANTHA: (*To audience*) I suppose this is as good a time as any to tell you... I'm a cat. Hence the twenty siblings. I hated them all. Mostly because they were all

mean to me and wouldn't let me eat. After a few
months of this I was really really thin and sickly.
I was probably on my last leg.

Think Ben Kingsley in Gandhi when he's close to the
end of the hunger strike...

What? You think just because I'm a cat I can't make
cultural references? Hello! I sit in front of the T V ninety
percent of my life, what do you expect?

Anyway, all my brothers and sisters had been given
away but because I was so little and scrawny nobody
wanted me. This was fine by me because it meant I had
my Mom all to myself.

But as it turned out, Mom always seemed to be busy
with the people of the house.

Then one night, Mom came to find me.

(MOM *appears. She's slightly out of breath.*)

MOM: There you are. I've been looking all over for you.

SAMANTHA: Mom! Hey!

MOM: Shhh... Keep your voice down.

SAMANTHA: Sorry.

MOM: Listen...I got a lot to tell you and a little bit of
time to do it. The woman of the house expects me in
the master bedroom in five minutes to watch *Cybil* on
the O Channel. And if I'm not there, she'll start to get
suspicious.

SAMANTHA: O K.

MOM: First, I want apologize for not being a good
mother.

SAMANTHA: No, you're a great—

MOM: No I'm not. I'm not a good mother. But I need
you to understand I'm a prisoner here. Practically every
second of my day is tied up with this family's lives and
schedules. And I hate this family. I've tried my whole

life to get away from them but never been able to.
They are not nice people. They have terrible taste in
furnishings. And they've never let me keep one kitten
from any of my litters. Not one!

SAMANTHA: But I'm still with you so maybe that means
they've changed.

MOM: They haven't.

SAMANTHA: But I don't understand—

MOM: Have they named you?

SAMANTHA: What do you mean?

MOM: Have they given you a name?

SAMANTHA: No. I don't think so. Not yet.

MOM: If they were going to keep you, trust me you'd
have a name by now.

SAMANTHA: But what's gonna happen to me?

MOM: You're going to be sent to the Animal Shelter.

SAMANTHA: The Animal Shelter? Don't they, you know
k-kill cats at the Shelter?

MOM: You get five days there. Five days to find
someone. And then... Lets not think about that.

SAMANTHA: Oh my god!

MOM: Shhh... Stay positive.

SAMANTHA: How am I supposed to stay positive about
this?

MOM: I need you think about this as an opportunity
to better your life. You have a chance to find someone
who will truly love you.

SAMANTHA: How am I going to do that?

MOM: You are simply not going to settle for anything
less. The biggest regret of my life is that when I was

sent to the Shelter, I was so terrified that I jumped at the first chance to get out. And now look at me. I'm trapped here. With people that don't know the difference between one hundred and eight hundred thread counts! I have refined tastes! I want better for you. I want you to find what I couldn't. True love.

Promise me you won't settle for anything less.

SAMANTHA: But—

MOM: Promise me. Please.

(Beat)

SAMANTHA: I promise.

MOM: Oh good. Good! This is good.

(Just then the theme song from Cybil *plays in the background.)*

MOM: Oh crap, *Cybil* is starting. I hate that show! *(She exits.)*

SAMANTHA: *(To audience)* The next day like Mom predicted I was sent to the Animal Shelter. It was totally horrible.
  Think *Amistad* meets *Schindler's List*
  I wanted to live up to my promise and find true love. But I didn't know how to go about it. How do you find your true love? Especially in an animal shelter where you only have five days to do it. But I tried not to think about this and instead focused on my goal. Find true love! Find true love! Find true love. The first time someone came by my cage, this is what happened.

(A SOUTHERN WOMAN comes up to SAMANTHA's cage.)

SOUTHERN WOMAN: *(With a southern accent)* As God as my witness I do declare I've never seen a more precious lil kitten in all the land.

SAMANTHA: I *am* precious! I'm yours! I love you! You love me! You're my true love! Take me home! I want to live every second of my life by your side!

SOUTHERN WOMAN: Heavens to Betsy, you simply won't do. I'm looking for a more self-sufficient cat. One that won't get in the way while I'm drinking my mint juleps. *(She exits.)*

SAMANTHA: *(To audience)* Self-sufficient. O K. I can be self-sufficient. I decided that the next time I'd show the person how self-sufficient I am.

(A FABULOUS MAN comes by SAMANTHA's cage.)

FABULOUS MAN: Girl! You are one fierce little kitten! Work it girl!

SAMANTHA: Thanks, but I don't really need you to tell me to work it. I'll work it all on my own.

FABULOUS MAN: Oh no! No, no no! You will not do! In my Technicolor world I need a cat that needs me to tell it what to do!

(With a snap of the fingers, FABULOUS MAN exits.)

SAMANTHA: *(To audience)* O K, so I can't be too needy, I need to be somewhat self-sufficient but also wanting to be told what to do. Ok, I can do this. I know I can.

(A DEPRESSED WOMAN enters.)

SAMANTHA: Hi, I'm looking for my one true love but if I don't find my one true love I'll be O K on my own unless you tell me you want me to be upset or something. I'll be whatever you want me to be, but only when it suits me...and you of course, I'll always take into consideration your feelings and—

DEPRESSED WOMAN: My life has no meaning.

SAMANTHA: I don't think this is really going to work out. *(To audience)* I was distraught. This was only my first day! After several more days of fruitless attempts, I was at my wits end, maybe my Mom was wrong, maybe I shouldn't have been so intent on finding true love. The thought just made me burst into tears. And it was at that exact moment that Shuman fell into my life.

   I don't mean to be dramatic, well yes I do, but this would be a good time for really romantic music. A great love song please.

(Wildly inappropriate music plays. Think...Baby Got Back or Who Let the Dogs Out*)*

SAMANTHA: Hey! HEY!

(The record should probably scratch here.)

SAMANTHA: That's not even a love song! Can we try that again please?
   A great love song please.

(The chorus of Olivia Newton John's I Honestly Love You *plays.)*

SAMANTHA: Hey!

(The record scratches again.)

SAMANTHA: So yes, that's a great love song but it's a little too slow and sappy for this moment. I think it should be a great love song that's happy and fun and thrilling! Got it? O K, one more time. A great love song please!

(Paul McCartney's Silly Love Song *plays.)*

SAMANTHA: That'll do. Thanks. *(To audience)* Anyway, O K, this is what happened. Shuman walked in.

*(*SHUMAN *enters.)*

SAMANTHA: *(To audience)* From across the crowded shelter our eyes met.

(He sees Samantha. They look at each other.)

SAMANTHA: *(To audience)* BAM! A connection!
It knocked us both off our feet! Like so.

(They both fall backwards.)

SAMANTHA: *(To audience)* Then, he got up, walked to
my cage, the door miraculously opened and a second
later I was in his arms. He was so warm and strong.
And then he put his hand under my chin and started
scratching and I, for the first time in my life, started to
purr.

SHUMAN: You're purring. Are you happy?

SAMANTHA: Yes very. *(To audience)* And if I didn't know
then that he was my true love. What he said next sealed
the deal.

SHUMAN: Hi. I guess you're coming home with me.
You're beautiful. Your name is... *(He looks deep into her
eyes for a moment)* Samantha. I know it is.

SAMANTHA: *(To audience)* Shuman named me.

SHUMAN: You don't have to be scared anymore, I'll love
you like you are supposed to be loved until the day I
die.

SAMANTHA: *(To audience)* And with that I dug my claws
deep into his sweater and wouldn't let go. And Shuman
took me to his home.

*(SHUMAN takes SAMANTHA into his house—very "carried
over the doorway". This should be a clear moment—a change
in the story as we move into SHUMAN's home for the first
time...fun pop music should play.)*

SAMANTHA: *(To audience)* Shuman's house sits deep in
a forest and from every window in every room all you
can see are trees and sky and grass.

SHUMAN: So this is home.

SAMANTHA: I love it Shuman!

SHUMAN: I'm so happy you're here! (*He rushes off.*)

SAMANTHA: (*To audience*) And Shuman became my true love. And it was everything I dreamed it would be. For a while at least. But we'll get to that later.

(*We are now in* SHUMAN'*s house. In his bedroom. In his bed, for that matter.*)

SAMANTHA: This is Shuman's bed.
   From the very first night I was home, I slept in it with Shuman. Some of you may think this was really quick, but it just felt so natural. Here's how it happened.

(SHUMAN *appears and gets into the bed.* SAMANTHA *stands in the doorway. The two look at each other. Then—*)

SHUMAN: Hey.

SAMANTHA: Hey.

SHUMAN: I'm going to sleep.

(*She stares. Beat*)

SHUMAN: Well...uh, goodnight.

SAMANTHA: Goodnight.

(*He turns off the light. Beat. He turns the light back on. The two stare at each other another moment. Then—*)

SHUMAN: Hey.

SAMANTHA: Hey.

SHUMAN: Uh—do you want to—uh—

SAMANTHA: (*To audience*) And before he even finished his sentence, I jumped onto the bed and crawled right in the crook of his arm, aka, armpit. (*She places herself under* SHUMAN'*s armpit. To audience*) And he turned off the light and we went to sleep. Here's what happened in the morning.

(*It's now morning.* SAMANTHA *watches* SHUMAN *sleep.*)

SAMANTHA: *(To* SHUMAN*)* You sleep restless. You look ugly in the morning. You have terrible breath. You hog the sheets. And the bed..... At least you don't fart.

(He farts.)

SAMANTHA: Ew...You're warm though. I like this bed. The sheets are comfy and really bright. They make me want to dig my claws into them. And into you. I'm so into you. You're cool. Do you like me? You can't hear me. You're not listening. Oh look at your hair, it's so clean and nice. I'm gonna lick your hair. Is that O K? I don't care. I want to and I'm going to. I'm going to lick your hair with flair. *(She does.)* Hmmm. Salty... Thick... I wanna lick it flat. Oh wow yeah. Oh yeah.

(Suddenly the alarm clock goes off. It's really loud, abrasive.)

SAMANTHA:AH!!!
(She literally jumps away.)

SHUMAN: Ah alarm!

SAMANTHA: Good morning.

SHUMAN: Hey there Samantha.

SAMANTHA: Hey.

(He turns over, going back to sleep.)

SAMANTHA: You're going back to sleep? You just got up and I'm hungry!

SHUMAN: Shhh.

SAMANTHA: Shhh? I'm hungry! Get up!

SHUMAN: Samantha, relax. Come here.

SAMANTHA: No.

SHUMAN: Come on.

(He grabs her and pulls her into him.)

SAMANTHA: But I'm hungry.

SHUMAN: Shhh....

SAMANTHA: Oh you feel good. I love the way you touch me. You've got great hands.

(SAMANTHA *rolls over on to her back. He rubs her belly and legs.*)

SHUMAN: You little slut.

SAMANTHA: Shut up, it feels good.

SHUMAN: Shhh. Sleep. Sleep.

SAMANTHA: O K, just keep touching me and I'll— (*She falls immediately sleep. Beat. Then she opens her eyes and turns to the audience.*) Before we go any further, I think that this may be a good time to tell you more on Shuman, the man.

(*We are now in* SHUMAN's *office.*)

SAMANTHA: Shuman works from home, doing web design, which sounds interesting and boring at the same time. In case you didn't notice, Shuman is very sensitive and cries over almost anything. Like so.

(SHUMAN *at his computer.*)

SHUMAN: Save. Save! SAVE! SAVE!!!! Why won't you save? I, I, I, I— (*He starts crying hysterically*).

SAMANTHA: Every morning Shuman gets up and talks to himself in the mirror. Like so.

(SHUMAN *stands looking at himself in the mirror.*)

SHUMAN: I am worthy of success. I am worthy of love. I am worthy of solitude. I am worthy of hope. I am worthy of dreams. I am worthy of time. I am worthy of Samantha. I am worthy of this day. Good morning.

SAMANTHA: And at night he has to brush his hair a hundred times before going to sleep. Like so.

(SHUMAN *stands looking at himself in the mirror and brushing his hair.* SAMANTHA *watches in awe.*)

SHUMAN: Ninety-eight, ninety-nine, one hundred. There. One hundred strokes. Goodnight.

SAMANTHA: *(To audience)* A big thing to Shuman is music. He loves it. And plays it in the house all the time. He only seems to like to play British pop songs from the eighties—Culture Club, Thompson Twins, Howard Jones and every other one or two hit wonder that tried to make it big in America. Anyway, one of Shuman's favorite things to do is put on music really loud and sing and dance to it. I am his audience and biggest fan. Sometimes he even lets me dance with him. Like so.

(SHUMAN *enters.*)

SHUMAN: Everybody dance!

(SHUMAN *performs an excerpt from Madness' song* Our House. *By the end of the song,* SHUMAN *has* SAMANTHA *in his arms and the two are dancing together.*)

SHUMAN: Our house in the middle of our street
Our house in the middle of our...
Our house...

SAMANTHA: *(To audience)* I guess the first time I noticed something wasn't quite right between Shuman and me was over dinner a couple months after I moved in.

(*The two sit across from each other at a table.*)

SHUMAN: You look pretty tonight.

SAMANTHA: Thanks Shuman. You look very nice too.

SHUMAN: After dinner do you wanna cuddle up in front of the T V and watch a movie?

SAMANTHA: O K.

SHUMAN: *Breakfast at Tiffany's* is on A M C tonight.
I love that movie. I saw that with my Mom... before she
died. Not right before she died, not on her deathbed or
anything. When I was little, she took me, to a revival of
it. But she's dead now. All my relatives are dead. Dead,
dead, dead, dead, dead, dead, dead.

SAMANTHA: I'm sorry Shuman.

(SHUMAN *begins to cry.* SAMANTHA *goes to comfort*
SHUMAN.)

SHUMAN: Oh Sammy! You are the greatest thing that's
ever happened to me!

SAMANTHA: *(To audience)* And it was at this exact
moment that I noticed Shuman had a crumb of food
on his upper lip. Shuman noticed me staring at him
and then he started staring at me and then he said—

SHUMAN: I wonder what you're thinking...

SAMANTHA: You have a crumb sticking on your upper
lip.

(SHUMAN *stares at* SAMANTHA *intently.*)

SHUMAN: You're trying to look into my soul aren't you?

SAMANTHA: No...I'm not. *(To audience)* So then I tried to
wipe it off with my paw. And Shuman said—

(She tries to wipe it off by rubbing his face with her paw.)

SHUMAN: Well I love you too.

(SHUMAN *then grabs* SAMANTHA's *paw and kisses it.)*

SAMANTHA: Ew. *(She pulls away.)*

SHUMAN: Alright, play coy Miss Sammy, I know you
love me.

SAMANTHA: Well I do love you but the point is you
have a crumb on your lip and its driving me crazy!...
(To audience) And for the first time I realized that maybe

Shuman didn't always understand me.

Just as clarification, I think I should say, I don't really speak in English. I speak in Cat. This is what I really sound like.

Meow wowo, memeo, meowwww, moeoem, moew.

So I suppose it shouldn't be all that surprising that Shuman didn't always understand me but still, sometimes he'd be so far off the mark it'd be shocking!

Like this one time, Shuman was working at his desk and I was so upset by something I saw on T V and needed to talk to him about it. Here's what happened.

(SHUMAN *is at his desk.* SAMANTHA *is at the door.*)

SAMANTHA: Hey.

SHUMAN: Hey Sammy.

SAMANTHA: This show I just saw was really disturbing.

(*No response from* SHUMAN *who keeps working.*)

SAMANTHA: It was on I F C or Sundance or Bravo— I can't tell the difference, I'm just a cat, and was a documentary about this filmmaker—

SHUMAN: I already fed you Sammy.

SAMANTHA: I know you fed me. Can you listen to me though for a sec? The filmmaker was trying to raise money for a film and kept running into all these problems and -

SHUMAN: Sammy! I can't play right now.

SAMANTHA: I know you can't play, I just want you to—

SHUMAN: SHHH!!!!

SAMANTHA: Don't shush me! I'm really upset!

SHUMAN: Sammy, I'm working!

SAMANTHA: Don't take that tone with me!

SHUMAN: Do you need to take a nap?

SAMANTHA: No.

SHUMAN: Do you have a hairball?

SAMANTHA: No! God! It's not a hairball!

SHUMAN: Hmmm…You look O K.

SAMANTHA: I am O K. My body is O K. It's my mind. I'm very emotional right now. I just need to talk.

SHUMAN: Sammy if you can't be quiet, I'm going to have to close the door.

SAMANTHA: Don't close the door. Just listen to me. Let me just tell you about this documentary—

SHUMAN: I'm sorry Sammy but I'm trying to work.

(SHUMAN *shuts the door on* SAMANTHA.)

SAMANTHA: Let me in Shuman. Shuman? Please? I just want to talk. Why won't you talk to me? Shuman? SHUMAN?…
    And soon other things became complicated for me as well—like when he'd go out for long periods of time without any real explanation.

(SHUMAN *exits.*)

SAMANTHA: And I wouldn't know when he'd be back or if he was coming back at all. The first few times he came back, I tried to act cool about it.

(SHUMAN *walks through the door.*)

SHUMAN: Hey Sammy.

SAMANTHA: Oh hey. Didn't hear you come in. Yeah, I was real busy by myself, uh huh. (*To audience*) But when he didn't tell me where he'd been or why he'd left, I'd want to lash out at him. But since he hadn't done anything wrong I had no reason to lash out, so I wouldn't. But then it happened again. And again. And again. Until one day, he walked in the door and I couldn't hold back anymore.

(SHUMAN *walks through the door.*)

SHUMAN: Hey Sammy.

SAMANTHA: Where were you? What were you doing? Who were you with? Why were you gone so long? Why didn't you take me? Why did you need to leave? I've been so scared and lonely and I thought you'd left me and were never coming back and I hate being alone even for a minute, you know that. You just left. Tell me where you went. Tell me!!!!!

SHUMAN: Someone sure is talkative today!

(SHUMAN *kisses* SAMANTHA *on the head and exits.*)

SAMANTHA: The next time he went out, I worked myself into such a frenzy that I started to feel really sick. My stomach hurt and my head ached and my legs felt all shaky and I was having a hard time breathing...
  Think Julia Roberts in *Steel Magnolias* right before she has her first seizure.
  Shuman found me later that day.

(SHUMAN *enters.*)

SHUMAN: There you are. I've been looking all over for you.

SAMANTHA: You have?

SHUMAN: Come on Sammy, lets go in the other room.

(SHUMAN *tries to pick* SAMANTHA *up. She won't budge.*)

SAMANTHA: I don't want to go anywhere. Leave me alone.

SHUMAN: Come on. Let me pick you up.

SAMANTHA: No.

SHUMAN: Why won't you let me pick you up?

SAMANTHA: Because I want to stay here.

SHUMAN: Are you ok?

SAMANTHA: No. I'm not ok. Go away.

(SHUMAN *looks at* SAMANTHA.)

SHUMAN: You're heart is racing Sammy, you're breathing is strange, you're, oh my god, you're sick! Oh Sammy! I—I—I—I don't know what to do, I—I—I—I think we're going to have to take you to the vet. I don't have a vet. I'll find a vet. Don't worry, I'll find someone to take care of you.

(*He's crying and then tries to pick* SAMANTHA *up.*)

SAMANTHA: No. No vet. Just leave me alone for awhile, I'll be fine.

SHUMAN: Shhh...They'll take care of you. Come on.

(SHUMAN *finally lifts* SAMANTHA *into his arms.*)

SAMANTHA: *(To audience)* So Shuman took me to the vet and that's where we met Matilda.

(MATILDA *sits at a desk on the phone. She's on the verge of tears.*)

MATILDA: *(Talking on the phone)* The thing is, Doctor Schaeffer, I just feel so lost. So terribly terribly lost. O K. I'll try that.

(SHUMAN *and* SAMANTHA *enter the vet's office.*)

MATILDA: Right now? But—O K, *(Reciting a mantra)* "I trust in the universe to guide me." I did too mean it. O K. "I trust in the universe to guide me". O K. Yes. That felt a little better. Thank you. *(She hangs up. Turning to* SHUMAN*)* Hello. How can I help you?

SHUMAN:—uh—Hello. My cat is sick and I don't know what to do.

MATILDA: Of course you don't. That's why you're here. At the vet. We take care of sick animals here.

SHUMAN: I know.

MATILDA: Good! That's the first step. Knowing. So just fill out this paperwork *(She hands* SHUMAN *a clipboard.)* and when its complete, bring it back to me. And then we'll go from there.

SHUMAN: O K...

*(*SHUMAN *sits with* SAMANTHA *and starts doing paperwork.)*

MATILDA: *(To herself)* I trust in the universe to guide me. I trust in the universe to guide me.

SAMANTHA: I want to go Shuman.

SHUMAN: Sammy shh...

SAMANTHA: I'm fine. I'll be fine.

SHUMAN: Sammy!

SAMANTHA: Please Shuman, just take me home!

MATILDA: It won't be that bad sweetie, I promise.

SHUMAN & SAMANTHA: Thanks.

SHUMAN: I am a little nervous. I guess I—

MATILDA: Actually I was talking to your cat. Oh my god, I was talking to your cat! *(To* SAMANTHA*)* Hi! I think I heard you. But to be sure can you speak again?

SAMANTHA: What should I say?

MATILDA: Anything you want to. Oh. Oh my, I heard you!

SAMANTHA: You did!*(To audience)* She did! Matilda could hear me! I liked her immediately.

MATILDA: My dream! This is—wow! That mantra really worked quick!

SHUMAN: Uh—

MATILDA & SAMANTHA: Shhh...

SHUMAN: But—

MATILDA: Hi, I'm Matilda.

SAMANTHA: I'm Samantha.

SHUMAN: I'm Shuman.

MATILDA: What's the matter sweetheart?

SAMANTHA: Well, I don't know, I'm just feeling really sick to my stomach and a little out of control. It's really complicated and I feel a little weird talking about it in front of *him*, if you know what I mean.

MATILDA: Yes I do know exactly what you mean Samantha. Hold on. *(To* SHUMAN*)* Well Shuman, it's clear that Samantha is going to have to stay overnight so you can just go now and I'll—

SHUMAN: Overnight?

MATILDA: Yes.

SHUMAN: But what's wrong?

MATILDA: I'm not at liberty to say. But it looks serious.

SAMANTHA: Serious?

MATILDA: Shh!

SHUMAN: You didn't even examine her. How do you know something's wrong? Are you the Doctor?

MATILDA: Well, no I'm not the Doctor. I'm the front desk girl, woman, womangirl. The Doctor is out of the office this afternoon, in a "meeting" if you catch my drift, very inappropriate, but who am I to judge? No one apparently, just the front desk womangirl, I have no opinions. Oh no, not Matilda. No, I'm just here to serve you, you selfish son of a— Anyway, he'll be back later. So I can just check Samantha in and then he'll see her later and examine her and determine precisely what's wrong.

SHUMAN: But she has to stay all night?

MATILDA: Yes.

SHUMAN: But we've never spent a night apart. I don't want her to be traumatized by it. Maybe I could stay and wait for the Doctor.

MATILDA: It'll be hours before he gets back.

SHUMAN: That's O K.

MATILDA: He works alone.

SHUMAN: I won't stand over him.

MATILDA: He doesn't like to be pressured.

SHUMAN: Maybe I should get a second opinion.

MATILDA: On what?

SHUMAN: On whether she should stay or not.

MATILDA: Samantha must stay.

SHUMAN: I just don't—I—well, I, I, I— *(Beat. He starts to cry.)*

MATILDA: Oh my. It's O K. Let it all out. It's O K.

SHUMAN: This is just—she's never been away from the house for the night and I don't want her to be lonely and sad and...I just love her so much and I don't want to lose her and—

MATILDA: Shuman, you're not going to lose her tonight, O K? I promise. I really want you to take a leap of faith here, O K?

(Beat)

SHUMAN: O K.

MATILDA: O K. Good.
  Now, have you finished filling out that paperwork?

(SHUMAN *bends down to fill out the paperwork.*)

SAMANTHA: *(To audience)* As soon as Shuman was gone,
Matilda turned to me and said—

MATILDA: The Doctor is gone for the rest of the night.
I lied to Shuman. I wanted to be alone with you.
  You see, Samantha, I've been having this recurring
dream that I can speak to cats. For almost two years.
Every night, the same dream. I'm sitting across from a
cat having a delicious Nicoise Salad and we're talking
and I'm giving the cat really smart advice. But I never
understood why.
  And then you come in today, and I can hear you
speak and I think you're what I've been waiting for
and I think I'm here to help you.
  And I'd like to help you, if you'd let me.

SAMANTHA: I'd like that.

MATILDA: Oh! Good! O K! O K! Good! Now! TELL ME
EVERYTHING!!!!

SAMANTHA: *(To audience)* And so I did. And we stayed
up all night, talking about Shuman and Matilda helped
me see that maybe I wasn't over-reacting at all but that
maybe—well, it's better when she says it. Listen.

MATILDA: I just think Samantha that you've made
Shuman too much of your life. You have to take space
for yourself. You have to find out who you are, you
know? He'll love you more if you do. Trust me, I know
this from experience. Like that guy Anthony, the one
I told you about? He loved me more when I stopped
dressing like him, calling him ten times a day and
peering into his windows with my high tech binoculars.
Sure, it took a restraining order to enforce that, but I
know deep down, he loves me more and to this day,

I know he wants me, he just hasn't been able to say it yet. But he will say it. One day. I'm certain of it. And until then I just have to keep breathing. Oh Anthony. Oh my, I've got to breathe. *(Does Lamaze breathing)* I'm taking Lamaze classes for the breathing exercises. I have a hard time breathing sometimes...I thought Lamaze would help, but I'm not sure if it is.

SAMANTHA: *(To audience)* O K, so maybe Matilda wasn't the most well adjusted person herself but still, she made some sense. I mean, really, I really did consume myself with Shuman's life. I made a vow then and there that when I got back home I would work really hard at finding out who I was and what made me tick and stop worrying so much about him.

In the morning when Shuman came to pick me up, Matilda stood by my side in a show of fierce sisterhood.

(SHUMAN enters.)

SHUMAN: Samantha! I missed you so much!

SAMANTHA: I missed you too!

MATILDA: Samantha!

SAMANTHA: But not as much as I thought I would.

MATILDA: Good girl. *(To SHUMAN)* Good morning Shuman.

SHUMAN: Hi.

MATILDA: You'll be pleased to know Samantha is all better.

SHUMAN: Oh that's great. What was wrong?

MATILDA: Well as it turns out, it seems Samantha's problems were mostly mental.

SHUMAN: I'm sorry?

MATILDA: Mental. As in "of the mind". You see, Shuman, Samantha and I spoke at length about this

last night and well, this is awkward but she feels
Shuman that you don't always listen to her.

SHUMAN: Uh— O K, I—

MATILDA: Actually, I wanted to give you my card,
in case you wanted me to come work with you both,
to work through your issues.

(MATILDA *hands* SHUMAN *a card. He looks it over.*)

SHUMAN: Cat therapist? I didn't know there was such
a thing.

MATILDA: It's a legitimate career path! (*Referring to the
card*) Do you like the little flowers I put around the
edges?

SHUMAN: Uh—

MATILDA: Don't answer that. I put all my various
numbers, emails and my home address on the card
for your and Samantha's convenience. I highly
recommend therapy Shuman. I'd hate to see things
fall apart.

SAMANTHA: She's really smart Shuman.

MATILDA: Oh that's so sweet Samantha! Thank you!

SHUMAN: What'd she say?

MATILDA: She said I was really smart.

SHUMAN: ...Right. O K, thanks for the card.

MATILDA: Please, I'm available any time. Any time
at all. And I make house calls of course. So call me.
This is the time to address these issues. Not later. Oh!
That sounds so official!

SHUMAN: Uh— O K.

MATILDA: Ok. Good. Very good. So I'll be hearing from
you both soon, I'm sure.

SHUMAN: Right.

(SHUMAN *picks up* SAMANTHA.)

MATILDA: Goodbye Samantha. Remember everything we talked about!

(MATILDA *grabs* SAMANTHA *and hugs her.*)

SAMANTHA: *(To audience)* And then we left. And came home. And I knew I had to stick to my vow and really give myself the space I needed. During the day, I was fine, nights though were really hard. We'd get into bed together like we always had before.

(*They get into bed.* SAMANTHA *under* SHUMAN's *arm.*)

SAMANTHA: And within seconds, Shuman would be fast asleep and I would be so wide awake I didn't know what to do with myself. With his arm around me I felt completely trapped. I could barely breathe. I wanted out of there immediately. So I'd try to move.

(*She tries to move.* SHUMAN *won't let go.*)

SAMANTHA: But the more I'd move the tighter his grip seemed to get.

   Then one night, I heard a rustling in the kitchen and I had to see who or what it was. After several failed attempts, I finally got out from under Shuman's arm and ran into the kitchen and found a mouse rifling through the cabinets.

(*A* MOUSE *appears. Think...Speedy Gonzalez.*)

MOUSE: Oh shit, a cat.

SAMANTHA: *(To audience)* No one had ever told me about mice before, but somehow I instinctively knew that mice were evil and that I was to rid the house of them. So that's what I did. Or attempted to do. All night long. Like so.

(SAMANTHA *chases the* MOUSE *all around the house to a fabulous and energetic soundtrack.*)

SAMANTHA: *(To audience)* Finally after much back and forth, I got the mouse under my paw, like so.

MOUSE: Ow.

SAMANTHA: Shut up. *(To audience)* And I started toying with it. Like so. *(To* MOUSE*)* Should I let you go?

MOUSE: Yes, please, I didn't mean to be here anyway, I must have taken a wrong turn in Albuquerque—

SAMANTHA: O K.

MOUSE: Oh thank you. Thank you. *(Starts to go.)*

SAMANTHA: Naw, changed my mind.

MOUSE: NO!!!!!

SAMANTHA: YES!!!!! *(To audience)* For those of you that are weak of heart, I'll refrain from illustrating the rest of what happened. For those of you that aren't weak of heart, think *Texas Chainsaw Massacre* meets *Nightmare on Elm Street's 1, 2, 3, 4* and...6!

(The MOUSE *disappears.)*

SAMANTHA: However, suffice it to say, eventually I killed it. This was an entirely new experience for me. Killing. Chasing. Using my instincts like that. It came so naturally. And it felt so good! I mean, really good! I felt like a wild tigress! And I never wanted to feel any different!

The whole next day I carried the mouse around with me in my mouth. The mouse changed everything about me. I started to walk with more confidence. Like so.

(Confident and sexy and sassy music plays think Right Said Fred's I'm Too Sexy. SAMANTHA *shows us her more confident walk.)*

SAMANTHA: *(To audience)* And then I noticed that my voice changed too. Like so. *(In her "stronger" voice, the mouse is now tucked under her arm)* I AM TIGRESS HEAR ME ROAR!!!! ROAR!!!! ROAROW!!!!!! *(To audience)* Later that day, I decided to show the new me to Shuman. *(She enters* SHUMAN's *office, mouse in mouth. She struts in.)* Shuman! Turn around and look at me I say!

SHUMAN: I'm working Sammy.

SAMANTHA: Turn around I say! ROAROW!!! ROAROW!!!!!!

SHUMAN: Sammy!

SAMANTHA: Fine! I'll come to you then. *(She gets onto his desk, mouse in hand [so to speak].)*

SHUMAN: What are you holding?

SAMANTHA: It's a mouse Shuman. My first! I killed it, violently last night, in a horrible bloody fight that took all night. Would you like to see it?

(SAMANTHA puts it on the desk so SHUMAN can examine it.)

SHUMAN: Oh Sammy...

SAMANTHA: Isn't it just divine?

SHUMAN: Oh my god...

SAMANTHA: I know. I know.

SHUMAN: This is so...disgusting.

SAMANTHA: What?

SHUMAN: Ew. Oh my god. Ew. Ew. Ew. I, I, I, I, I,—

(SHUMAN starts to slide the mouse off the desk, presumably into a trash can. SAMANTHA blocks him.)

SAMANTHA: What are you doing?

SHUMAN: Sammy, let go, the mouse has to be thrown away.

SAMANTHA: NO!

SHUMAN: Samantha, let go of the mouse.

SAMANTHA: No! The mouse is mine. I killed it. You can't just throw it away. Its mine! MINE!

(SHUMAN *then picks* SAMANTHA *up and moves her. She flails.*)

SAMANTHA: No! SHUMAN GET OFF ME! LET ME GO! THE MOUSE IS MINE! GIVE ME BACK MY MOUSE! *(To audience)* But he didn't listen to me and he threw the mouse away. After that I snuck out of bed every night and roamed the house looking for danger or excitement or both.

And then one night, while stalking through the kitchen, the very thing I'd been looking for found me. And his name was Oscar the cat.

(OSCAR *the Cat appears in a haze of smoke. He is one cool cat. Sexy R & B plays [Think R Kelly]*)

SAMANTHA: *(To audience)* I first spotted him through the sliding glass door. I was frozen to the spot. I couldn't move. I couldn't breathe.

OSCAR: Hey...sup sweetheart?

SAMANTHA: *(To audience)* I couldn't speak. All I could do was watch and listen.

OSCAR: What's the matter cat got your tongue? ...That's a joke, get it? Cat? ...Skip it. ...Hey...I'm Oscar. I'm an alley cat. Moved up here from the city a few years back. All the hustle and bustle just got to me one day and I took off. It's nice up here. Quiet. But I'll tell you what... a little boring. That is until I spotted you. Yeah, I'm not ashamed to admit it. I've had my eye on you for a while now. You are one sexy kitten. I've been trying to figure

out how old you are. I'm guessing, a year? Am I right?
Maybe a little less? Wanna give me a hint here? ...So are
you acting cool or are you shy? I hope you're shy cause
I hate cool. I'm not into playing games. I just say what
I feel...how about you? Nothing huh?

   Well I tried. How about I come by tomorrow and try
again? Say, same place, same time? ...I'll take that for a
yes. Later baby. *(He exits.)*

SAMANTHA: *(To audience)* And we fell into a pattern.
Every night Oscar would show up, try to get me to talk,
he'd fail, he'd talk about himself and then leave. I'd
be breathless for him the whole next day and then one
night, a few weeks later he took things to a new level.

(OSCAR appears again.)

OSCAR: So... do you ever speak? I think you do. But
if you didn't I'd still like you. Yeah O K, I like you.
So what? I like you. Do you like me?

SAMANTHA: *(To audience)* I wanted to answer but I was
scared.

OSCAR: You could at least nod your head or something.
Up and down if you like me, side to side if you don't.

SAMANTHA: *(To audience)* So I nodded my head up and
down, like so. *(She does.)*

OSCAR: I knew it!... I mean, that's cool... No I don't,
I mean—COOL! You're cool. Do you like living inside?
I've never done it. Can't imagine what's it like. Outside
is the only place I've ever lived. Born and bred. If you
ever got out here, I'd show you all these cool places
around here. Like there's a little garden just down the
road that I like to stalk in. And around the corner over
there, there's the most comfortable patch of grass. In
the afternoon I lay out there and get sun. Have you ever
felt sun on your coat? It's heaven. I can't imagine not
having felt that. You have to feel that. It's natural. Its

what you're supposed to feel. I'm babbling. I'm gonna go. *(He leaves. Then re-enters.)* See ya tomorrow sweetheart. *(He leaves again.)*

SAMANTHA: *(To audience)* After he left all I could think about was what it must be like to feel the sun on your coat. And I started to wonder why hadn't Shuman ever taken me outside? Why was I an indoor cat? The next night Oscar talked more about his life outside.

OSCAR: Don't get me wrong. It's not always a picnic out here. I mean, tornadoes are no joke. But for the most part it's like a giant playground. Oh, which reminds me. I brought you a present. *(He takes out a gift-wrapped box.)* Just a little play-thing, something I saw and made me think of you. Nothing really. It's not a big deal or anything, just, alright I'm shutting up now... Well.. Open it! That's a joke. I know you can't open it. What's that? Oh you want me to open it for you? Well if you insist. O K. *(He opens the gift. He pulls out a pine cone.)* It's a pine cone. They fall from those trees over there. They're really fun to knock around. *(He demonstrates.)* I mean I don't know if you like knocking things around but I do and I figured maybe you did too but I don't really know but if you do, and if you ever were to come outside you could knock this around. Anyway, I'm just gonna leave it here for you.

SAMANTHA: *(To audience)* I'd never gotten a present before. Shuman never bought me anything, except things I needed. He would never think of just getting me something for fun. Or to show me how he felt about me. But Oscar. Oscar thought of me and got me something. Just for me. And if this wasn't enough, then he said something that really got to me.

OSCAR: You know where I wish I could take you? The beach. Do you know its only sand and water? Nothing else for as far as the eye can see. Can you imagine that? Just water and sand. It's like a giant litter box. And sand, oh man, sand is supposed to feel like heaven underneath your paws. I'm dying to feel that. Sure during the day people are around but at night, it'd be ours.

SAMANTHA: *(To audience)* Ours. He said ours. I'd never thought of there being another "ours" besides me and Shuman and then there was Oscar saying "ours" and I couldn't help but think that it sounded right. Like I was really supposed to be with Oscar outside and not with Shuman inside. That Oscar and I were the right "ours" and Shuman and I weren't.

With Shuman love had always felt like a comfortable blanket wrapped around me. But with Oscar, it was inside me. Deep inside all the way to the core of me and was filling me up and any minute I was going to explode from it.

I wanted to give myself over to Oscar. I wanted to speak to Oscar. But I lived with Shuman. I loved Shuman. Or maybe I didn't. I didn't know anymore. I didn't feel like I knew anything anymore. I needed help. I needed clarity. I needed guidance. I needed... Matilda! Matilda would know what to do. But how was I going to get to her? And then I remembered that Matilda gave Shuman her card and I knew Shuman had put it on his desk when we got home that day.

So first I got her card off Shuman's desk. Then I knocked the phone out of its holder. *(She does all these things.)* Then, the tricky part. Dialing the number. Paws are great for a lot of things but they aren't exactly precise. Here's my first attempt at calling Matilda.

(SAMANTHA attempts to dial the number. We hear the phone ringing. Lights up on AMSTERDAM WOMAN.)

AMSTERDAM WOMAN: *Hallo! Leibenstrasse Huis!*

SAMANTHA: Matilda?

AMSTERDAM WOMAN: *Is dit een kattenkopje beslagen
en zoeterd? (Rough translation: Is this a little cat soft and
cuddly?)*

SAMANTHA: Uh...wrong number. *(To audience)* So I tried
again. I tried to dial the right numbers this time.

(Phone rings again. Lights up on MICHAEL JACKSON.*)*

MICHAEL JACKSON: Hello?

SAMANTHA: Matilda?

MICHAEL JACKSON: This is Michael Jackson. Is this a
little kitty cat?

SAMANTHA: Uh...yes, but I think I have the wrong
number.

MICHAEL JACKSON: *(Singing)* Eee-hee. Jam on! Jam on!

*(*MICHAEL JACKSON *moonwalks as* SAMANTHA *quickly
hangs up.)*

SAMANTHA: *(To audience)* This was really starting
to stress me out. I decided to try one more time.
(She dials again.).

(Phone rings again. Lights up on MATILDA*!!!!)*

MATILDA: Hello?

SAMANTHA: Matilda?

MATILDA: Samantha?

SAMANTHA: Matilda! Yes! It's me Samantha!

MATILDA: Oh Samantha! You have been on my mind
so much lately! WHO IS RASPUTIN?

SAMANTHA: What? Uh—I don't know, I—

MATILDA: Oh no, sorry Samantha, I'm watching
Jeopardy and sometimes I yell out the answers. Sorry.
I'm turning the T V off now. O K...I'm here for you
now. What's going on Samantha?

SAMANTHA: Well Matilda I have a really big problem and I need your advice. It's about Shuman and—

(Just then SHUMAN *walks in.)*

SHUMAN: Sammy? What are you doing?

SAMANTHA: Uh—

MATILDA: It's about Shuman and...what Samantha?

SHUMAN: How did you get the phone?

(SHUMAN *goes to pick up the phone.* SAMANTHA *tries to stop him. (Note: For the sake of rhythm, lines here should overlap.)*

SAMANTHA: Shuman, no!

SHUMAN: Sammy! Shhh! *(Into the phone)* Hello?

MATILDA: Put Samantha on the phone please.

SHUMAN: Excuse me.

SAMANTHA: Give me the phone!

MATILDA: Hello Shuman, this is Matilda, please put Samantha back on the phone.

SHUMAN: Matilda from the vet's office?

MATILDA: That's right.

SAMANTHA: Let me speak to her.

SHUMAN: *(To* SAMANTHA*)* Shhh... *(To* MATILDA*)*
I don't understand what's going on here.

MATILDA: Samantha called me, she needed to talk and—

SHUMAN: Uh—Samantha's—a cat.

MATILDA: Yes, and?

SAMANTHA: Shuman!!!

SHUMAN: *(To* SAMANTHA*)* Shhh! *(To* MATILDA*)*
She doesn't talk on the phone. She can't call people
on the phone.

SAMANTHA: Yes I can, I did! Please Shuman! Just leave
us alone for a few minutes!

SHUMAN: SAMMY! SHUT UP!

MATILDA: Don't you dare yell at her!

SHUMAN: I'm not.

MATILDA: Yes you are!

SHUMAN: She just—listen I have to go.

MATILDA: I'm concerned Shuman, I'm very—

SHUMAN: Right, good talking to you.

MATILDA: I WILL NOT SIT IDLY BY—

*(*SHUMAN *hangs up before* MATILDA *finishes.*
She disappears.)

SAMANTHA: Why wouldn't you let me talk to her?
I needed to talk to her! Why do you always butt in
on everything? Why can't you just give me space!

SHUMAN: Sammy—

(The phone starts ringing again. SHUMAN *lets it ring.*
Then he looks at SAMANTHA *and moves the phone far out*
of her reach.)

SAMANTHA: Answer it! It's Matilda! Answer it,
so I can speak to her! Answer the phone.

SHUMAN: Sammy calm down.

SAMANTHA: Don't tell me to calm down, I want
to speak to Matilda, please, she's calling for me.
I need her. You don't understand. You don't
understand anything about me!

SHUMAN: Just, Sammy, please, just be quiet. Quiet down. Please.

SAMANTHA: NO!!!!

SHUMAN: Jesus! Samantha what's the matter with you?

SAMANTHA: What's the matter with me? What's the matter with me? Everything's the matter! You're the matter!

SHUMAN: Are you sick or something?

SAMANTHA: UH!!!! Why won't you listen to me? Listen to me! Ugh! Just forget it!

(SAMANTHA *turns away from him.*)

SHUMAN: Please don't ignore me. Please.

SAMANTHA: I'm ignoring you.

SHUMAN: Please. Samantha! Please!

SAMANTHA: I said, I'm ignoring you!

SHUMAN: Fine... Then...I'm going out!

SAMANTHA: Fine!

SHUMAN: Fine! (*He storms out.*)

SAMANTHA: (*To audience*) As soon as he left, I went and found Oscar.

(OSCAR *appears.*)

SAMANTHA: I CAN SPEAK!!!!!

OSCAR: I knew it! I knew you did! Say some more.

SAMANTHA: What should I say?

OSCAR: I don't care. Recite the alphabet twenty times. Count backwards from a billion. Anything. Say anything.

SAMANTHA: Uh—hi.

OSCAR: That'll work.

SAMANTHA: My name's Samantha.

OSCAR: Samantha. Sa-man-tha. I like that. Samantha...
Hi Samantha. I'm Oscar. You already know that.
You know practically everything about me already.
I guess I've been talking a lot. But I haven't had much
choice have I? You got a lot of catching up to do.

SAMANTHA: Where should I start?

OSCAR: Wherever you want to.

(Beat)

SAMANTHA: Uh- I don't know. Ask me some questions.

OSCAR: What's your favorite position...to nap in..?

SAMANTHA: I like to curl up in a ball on the sofa.

OSCAR: I like to do that too! Not on the sofa, I mean
there aren't any sofas out here, but I like to curl up
in a ball too. That's how I take my naps. Just like that,
in a ball. What else?

SAMANTHA: I killed a mouse once.

OSCAR: You're a beast! You're a goddess! You're a
tigress! You're—you're so unbelievable! You're—
Oh this is just too much! I'm overwhelmed here!
I'm freaking out Samantha! I'm freaking out. That's it.
I'm out of control. I gotta sing. I just gotta!

SAMANTHA: Sing?

OSCAR: I always sing when I'm freaking out. It...
focuses me. One! Two! One, two, three, four!!!!!

*(He bursts into song—something vibrant and rock-n-roll—
think Lenny Kravitz's* Fly Away. *Whatever the choice,
by the end of the song both* OSCAR *and* SAMANTHA *should
be really into it.)*

(Suddenly SHUMAN *enters the kitchen. He flips on a light.)*

SHUMAN: Samantha?

SAMANTHA: Uh—uh—uh—

SHUMAN: Who's this? What's going on?

SAMANTHA: Go away! Get out of here.

OSCAR: Who me?

SAMANTHA: No, not you Oscar! Him!

SHUMAN: Where'd she come from?

OSCAR & SAMANTHA: She?

SHUMAN: You two friends?

SAMANTHA: We're more than just friends. We're—

SHUMAN: That's so sweet.

SAMANTHA: It's not sweet, it's—

SHUMAN: O K Sammy, say goodnight to your little friend

OSCAR: Little? I'm not little, I'm—

SHUMAN: Come on, let's go to bed.

SAMANTHA: No.

SHUMAN: Night night little cutie!

SAMANTHA: I'm not going to bed with you Shuman.

SHUMAN: You want me to pick you up? O K.

(SHUMAN *picks* SAMANTHA *up in his arms.*)

SAMANTHA: Put me down. I want to stay here. I want to stay with Oscar!

SHUMAN: Calm down Sammy. Sammy stop wriggling. Sammy!

SAMANTHA: *(To audience)* And I was so angry at him for picking me up and disturbing me and Oscar that

I—well I did something I'd never done before...
I bit him. Hard. Like so.

(SAMANTHA *bites* SHUMAN's *arm.*)

SHUMAN: OW!!!! GOD DAMN IT!!!!!! OW!!!!!

(SAMANTHA *jumps out of* SHUMAN's *arms.*)

SAMANTHA: *(To* SHUMAN*)* HA! You deserve it!
You, you, you!!!!

SHUMAN: I—I—I—I—I—I—

SAMANTHA: *(Hissing at* SHUMAN*)* GET OUT OF HERE
NOW!!!!!!

SHUMAN: Samantha, I—I—I—

SAMANTHA: *(Still hissing)* NOW!!!!!!!

SHUMAN: I can't believe you bit me! Bad girl! Bad BAD
GIRL! You will not be allowed in bed tonight! You can
stay out here and think about what you did!

(SHUMAN *exits.* SAMANTHA *turns to* OSCAR.)

SAMANTHA: So, where were we?

OSCAR: ...I should probably go.

SAMANTHA: Oh.

OSCAR: I shouldn't be here right now.

SAMANTHA: Well I—no. I don't want you to, I—

OSCAR: Look, save your breath. I'm an alley cat, O K?
I know how this goes. So I'm just gonna back away
now. Real slow. And then it'll be like I wasn't ever
here and it'll all be cool. I mean it won't be cool.
It'll stink but I'll be fine. Eventually. *(He starts to leave.)*

SAMANTHA: No! Oscar! I love you.

OSCAR: You do?

SAMANTHA: Yes...I do. I love you! I LOVE YOU!
Do you love me?

OSCAR: Have since the moment I caught a glimpse of
that tail of yours. Love everything about you. Every
little hair and paw. Can't get enough of you. You got
me pussy whipped Samantha, excuse my vulgarity.

SAMANTHA: I kind of like it when you talk like that.
It makes me feel...wild. So wild that I can't stay inside
anymore. Oscar I want to bust out of here and live with
you for the rest of my life.

OSCAR: You do?

SAMANTHA: Yes! I'm nothing inside. I need to get to
you!

OSCAR: You're not playing a game are you?

SAMANTHA: No. I mean it. Do you want me to be with
you?

OSCAR: More than anything. I want you here with me.
I want you to be outside.

SAMANTHA: I'm going to get to you.

OSCAR: But how?

SAMANTHA: I don't know yet. But I'm going to figure
something out. I promise I am. *(To audience)* And the
whole time, he would look at me with those eyes!
Those eyes that made me feel like I was a beautiful
wild tigress. I could feel it in me, my wildness,
like my blood, coursing through me.
    And then that made me think that maybe if I started
to act wild around the house, Shuman would get the
idea and let me out.
    So I started doing these really complex and bizarre
running patterns all around the living room. Like so.

(SAMANTHA *indeed does a bizarre running pattern.*
SHUMAN *follows, talking as he runs.)*

SHUMAN: Sammy? Sammy! Stop! Hey!

(SAMANTHA *as she continues to run, speaks to the audience.*)

SAMANTHA: I then proceeded to destroy everything
I possibly could. Like so.

(*As she continues to run,* SAMANTHA *starts knocking off
plants, books, tables, chairs—anything and everything in her
way.* SHUMAN *attempts to pick up the pieces behind her.*)

SHUMAN: Stop it Sammy! *Samantha!* I—I—I—I— Hey!
No! That's expensive! Why are you doing this? Stop it!
Stop it Samantha!!!! Oh. O K. O K. You win. O K? You
win! Just go ahead. I'll clean up later. I—I need to sit.
I need to sit and...breathe. Oh god, do I need to breathe.
(*He sits and breathes.*)

SAMANTHA: (*To audience*) I knew I had to take things
further if I wanted Shuman to kick me out, but I didn't
know how to. How much more wild could I get?
I racked my brain over this for days and then finally
one morning while in my litter box, it hit me or rather,
dropped out of me. If you catch my drift...
    I decided that the best place to do it would be on his
computer. After all he spent so much time there and
it was his money line and he couldn't just wash it in
the washing machine. If I really did it right, he would
possibly have to get a whole new computer. So first,
I ate a lot of food in the kitchen and then waited until
I felt like I needed to go to the bathroom. Then I waited
until Shuman took a break to watch T V. His computer
was on and open and then I stood on top of it and—
well, here's exactly what I was thinking, in the moment.
    (*To herself*) O K Sammy. This is it. Just relax and
dump. Come on. Relax. Breathe in. Breathe out. Come
on Sammy. Just release. Release! Release! (*To audience*)
But I couldn't release. I couldn't stop thinking about
how much it was going to hurt Shuman and how much
I didn't want to hurt him. How all I wanted to do was

to be outside and why did that mean that I had to hurt
Shuman? And then I guess because I wasn't thinking
about going to the bathroom, I started to. Right there.
On the computer. And it was one of those things that
once I started I couldn't stop. And so I just steeled
myself and let it rip. Afterwards, I hid in a cabinet in
the kitchen and waited. And soon enough, Shuman
discovered it.

(SHUMAN *enters and sees the computer.*)

SHUMAN: No. Ew. SAMMY!!!!!??? I, I, I, I, I,!!!!!!

SAMANTHA: *(To audience)* So I left my hiding place and
went right up to him and stared at him with a look of
defiance.

(SHUMAN *picks* SAMANTHA *up.*)

SHUMAN: I've had it with you. Do you hear me?
I've had it! I hate you Samantha! I hate you! You've
destroyed everything in this house! You've practically
destroyed me! I'm throwing you out. Out into the forest
so you can get attacked and killed and eaten by wild
animals. So, goodbye! Goodbye! And don't come
back asking for food. Because I'm not giving you any.
I can only take so much and I've taken a lot from you
Samantha! A lot. But this, this was it! So... Goodbye.
Goodbye! *(He goes to open the door.)*

SAMANTHA: *(To audience)* We were so close. And then
Shuman opened the door and—

(SHUMAN *opens the door.* MATILDA *is there.*)

SAMANTHA & SHUMAN: Matilda!

MATILDA: That's right. Its me. Matilda. I told you I
would not sit idly by! And from what I can tell, that
was a good thing. Alright, step away from the door,
I'm coming in! *(Blackout)*

END OF ACT ONE

ACT TWO

(Lights up on MATILDA, SHUMAN *and* SAMANTHA *all sitting in the living room looking at each other.)*

SAMANTHA: *(To audience)* An hour after Matilda arrived, none of us had said a word to each other. Shuman was mad at me, Matilda was mad at Shuman and I was mad at both of them.... Then finally, Matilda said—

MATILDA: Would you two like to say hello to each other?

SHUMAN & SAMANTHA: No.

MATILDA: O K. Just testing the waters there. Icy cold, brrr! O K. So, it's obvious to me that there's been a complete breakdown in communication here. do you both agree?

(No answer)

MATILDA: I said do you both agree?

SHUMAN & SAMANTHA: Yes.

MATILDA: Good. Common ground has been established. O K. We're going to do an exercise to help us, us meaning you two, start to communicate to each other. The exercise is called "I Feel" and its really very simple. Both of you are going to sit in these two chairs I've placed opposite each other and one of you is going to start and simply say, "I Feel" and then add an emotion onto the end. Then the other says, "I feel" and says what they feel, O K?

SHUMAN: How am I going to know what Samantha's saying?

MATILDA: You are going to listen.

SHUMAN: But—

MATILDA: I said Shuman that you are going to listen!

SHUMAN: O K. Fine. Whatever.

MATILDA: Fine. Now both of you have a seat please.

(*They do.*)

MATILDA: Good. And who would like to start.
No, scratch that, Shuman you start.

(*Silence*)

SHUMAN: Matilda, this is stupid—

MATILDA: Uh uh, turn to Samantha and tell her how you feel. No emotion is wrong.

SHUMAN: Fine. I feel stupid.

MATILDA: Good Shuman! Good! Samantha?

SAMANTHA: I feel...impatient.

MATILDA: Good Samantha.

SHUMAN: What'd she say?

MATILDA: Listen to her. Samantha repeat yourself.

SAMANTHA: But I feel differently now.

MATILDA: Then say whatever you feel.

SAMANTHA: I feel frustrated.

MATILDA: Good. Shuman?

SHUMAN: I still don't understand.

MATILDA: Very well, I'll help you along for a bit.
She said she feels frustrated.

SHUMAN: Why?

MATILDA: Uh uh, "I feel..."

SHUMAN: I feel confused.

MATILDA: Good.

SAMANTHA: I feel trapped.

MATILDA: Try to stick with emotions. She said she feels trapped.

SHUMAN: I feel confused still.

SAMANTHA: I feel insignificant.

MATILDA: She feels insignificant.

SHUMAN: Why?

MATILDA: I feel...

SHUMAN: I feel questioning?

MATILDA: That'll work.

SAMANTHA: I feel unknown.

MATILDA: She said she feels unknown.

SHUMAN: I feel confused.

SAMANTHA: I feel you don't listen.

MATILDA: She feels you don't listen.

SHUMAN: Am I supposed to listen to her?

SAMANTHA: I feel like you refuse to know me.

MATILDA: She said she feels like you refuse to know her.

SHUMAN: Does she need to be known?

SAMANTHA: Yes.

MATILDA: Stick with "I feels" ...Shuman, start us up again.

SHUMAN: I feel like you think you can talk to cats!

MATILDA: I feel like I can. But this isn't about me.

SHUMAN: I feel like you should leave my house!

MATILDA: I feel like you're wrong. But again, this isn't about me.

SHUMAN: You can't just stay when I ask you to leave.

MATILDA: Yes I can. Continue please.

SHUMAN: I feel like this was fine without you here.

MATILDA: I feel like had I not arrived when I did, you would have thrown Samantha out of your house.

SHUMAN: I feel like that's my prerogative. Besides I would never have left her outside.

SAMANTHA: I feel like I would have been happy outside.

MATILDA: I feel like you don't know what you're talking about.

SHUMAN & SAMANTHA: Yes I do.

MATILDA: I feel confused.

SHUMAN: I feel out of the loop.

MATILDA: I feel like Samantha needs to clarify.

SAMANTHA: I wanted to get outside. I've been trying to get outside.

MATILDA: Why?

SAMANTHA: To be with Oscar.

MATILDA: Who's Oscar?

SHUMAN: Oscar?

MATILDA: Shhh.

SHUMAN: Who's Oscar?

MATILDA: Shuman, I'm putting you on time out.

SHUMAN: O K, this is it. Out! Get out of my house! I've tried. I don't know why but I tried. I tried to cooperate.

You saw me cooperate right? I tried. But this is
just absolutely ridiculous, you're talking to my cat.
You're trying to get me to talk to my cat.

MATILDA: And that makes you feel—?

SHUMAN: Silly! I feel silly!

MATILDA: Because?

SHUMAN: Because—she's—she's a cat! She doesn't—
she's not supposed to have all this stuff going on in her.
She's supposed to be simple. That's why I got a cat!
I wanted simple. I'm good at simple. I'm not good
at the other stuff. I can't. I can't give more than that.
I'm incapable of it. I've tried. I can't.

MATILDA: Good. I'm sensing anger.

SHUMAN: You're damn right your sensing anger! You!
You come in here! And take everything over and tell
me what I can and can't do and what's going on with
my cat! MY CAT! You have no right!

MATILDA: Good, go with this Shuman, let it all out!

SHUMAN: And I don't think you know anything! I think
you're making it all up! I think you're a looney tune!
YOU'RE A LOONEY TUNE DO YOU HEAR ME?
I hate you! I hate you Matilda! I hate you!

MATILDA: Well I hate you too! You're selfish! You're
over emotional and yet somehow insensitive! You're
a complete mess! A complete and utter mess! I've hated
you since the minute I met you!

SHUMAN: The feeling's mutual.

MATILDA: Oh yeah?

SHUMAN: Yeah!

(Beat. The two stare at each other. Fireworks)

MATILDA: Good. O K. Good. Good. So now Shuman I'm putting you on time out. O K?

SHUMAN: O K.

MATILDA: O K. Samantha, private conference with me over here.

SAMANTHA *follows* MATILDA *to another side of the room.*

MATILDA: Now, Samantha, where were we?

SAMANTHA: We were talking about Oscar.

MATILDA: Oscar. Right. Who's Oscar?

SAMANTHA: An alley cat. We're in love.

MATILDA: Oh my.

SAMANTHA: As soon as I get out of here, we're going away together. You ruined everything when you showed up. Shuman was just about to throw me out.

MATILDA: Oh my.

SAMANTHA: I'm not happy here Matilda. I don't want to make this work. I'm not meant to be an indoor cat. I'm an outdoor cat.

MATILDA: But how do you know?

SAMANTHA: I killed a mouse. I—I'm a wild tigress. I'm—

MATILDA: Oh my.

SAMANTHA: So you have to help me Matilda. You have to help me get out of here. Distract Shuman or something. Open the door for me. Let me be free to be with the cat I love! To be my true self. To love! To Live!

MATILDA: But what about Shuman?

SAMANTHA: I've been trying to get away from him ever since I got back from meeting you. He's bad for me. He doesn't care for me. He doesn't know me. I need to be known. I need to be—

MATILDA: Oh my.

SAMANTHA: So will you help me get out of here?

(Beat)

MATILDA: No. No Samantha I won't help you leave.

SAMANTHA: You won't?

MATILDA: No, I'm going to help you stay.

SAMANTHA: Why?

MATILDA: Because there's something worth fighting for here.

SAMANTHA: How can you say that? You have no idea what Oscar makes me feel, you have no idea how I've felt here. I feel compromised, I feel like— like I've settled. I don't want to settle Matilda.

MATILDA: How is staying and letting yourself be known to Shuman settling?

SAMANTHA: I feel like you don't understand me.

MATILDA: I feel like maybe you don't understand yourself.

(Quite suddenly, SAMANTHA *bites* MATILDA*.... Hard)*

MATILDA: OW!!!! Oh! You little... Samantha! Oh!!!!!

SHUMAN: What happened?

MATILDA: She bit me! Samantha you bit me!

SHUMAN: Samantha! Bad girl! Bad bad girl!

MATILDA: Yes bad girl. No. Not bad girl. That's bad to say. You're not a bad girl. You're just confused. You're lost. You're—I'm—I'm—I must, I must breathe. Breathe Matilda. *(She does some of the Lamaze breathing.)* Let's just

get this all out in the open. Shuman, Samantha is in love
with an alley cat named Oscar.

SAMANTHA: SHUMAN:
Matilda!   What?

MATILDA: And she wants to live outside with him.
How does that make you feel? Tell Samantha.

SHUMAN: I feel...confused. Overwhelmed. Unsure.
Is this true? Samantha? I—I—I—

SAMANTHA: It's true.

MATILDA: She said it's true.

SHUMAN: When did this happen? Where did you meet?
How could this happen?

SAMANTHA: It all just happened. It felt...natural.

MATILDA: She doesn't know how it happened.

SHUMAN: And you love him?

SAMANTHA: Yes.

MATILDA: She said yes.

SHUMAN: More than me?

SAMANTHA: I think so.

MATILDA: She said she thinks so.

SHUMAN: I feel like I don't understand.

SAMANTHA: I feel like you don't want to understand.

MATILDA: She feels you don't want to understand.

SHUMAN: If I knew you needed to be understood
I would have tried.

SAMANTHA: How could you think I didn't need to be?

MATILDA: How could you think she didn't need to be?

SHUMAN: I just thought she was simple.

SAMANTHA: I don't feel simple.

MATILDA: She doesn't feel simple.

SHUMAN: I feel bad.

SAMANTHA: I feel bad.

MATILDA: She said she feels—

(SHUMAN *stops* MATILDA *with his hand. Beat.* SHUMAN *really looks at* SAMANTHA, *he can hear her.*)

SHUMAN: I feel like I'm not enough.

SAMANTHA: I feel like I'm too much.

SHUMAN: I feel like no matter what I do you're not happy.

SAMANTHA: I feel like you never listen to me.

SHUMAN: I feel like I try to.

SAMANTHA: I feel like you do sometimes.

SHUMAN: I feel like sometimes I don't want to.

SAMANTHA: I feel like you're being honest.

SHUMAN: I feel like sometimes I get afraid.

SAMANTHA: I feel like sometimes I want more than you could give.

SHUMAN: I feel like I want to give you everything but don't know how to.

SAMANTHA: I feel like I want to give some things to myself.

SHUMAN: I feel like I never knew that.

SAMANTHA: I feel like I need to be known.

SHUMAN: I feel like I want to know you.

SAMANTHA: I feel like you can't ever know me.

SHUMAN: I feel like I'd like to try.

SAMANTHA: I feel like its too late.

SHUMAN: I feel like you're wrong.

SAMANTHA: I feel like you're wrong.

SHUMAN: I feel like you're being stubborn.

SAMANTHA: I feel like you're not listening to me.

SHUMAN: I feel like you're not letting me in.

SAMANTHA: I feel like you want to smother me.

SHUMAN: I feel like I just want to hold you.

SAMANTHA: I feel like I don't want to be held.

SHUMAN: I feel like you're afraid.

SAMANTHA: I feel like you're wrong.

SHUMAN: I feel like you want something from me I can't give you.

SAMANTHA: I feel like you could give it to me if you wanted.

SHUMAN: I feel like you want me to let you leave.

SAMANTHA: I do.

SHUMAN: I won't do that.

SAMANTHA: But that's what I want.

SHUMAN: I don't think you know what you want.

SAMANTHA: I don't think you know me well enough to know.

SHUMAN: I feel like we have a history together.

SAMANTHA: I feel like you want to live in the past.

SHUMAN: I feel like you want to live in the future.

SAMANTHA: I want to live with Oscar.

SHUMAN: I want to live with you.

SAMANTHA: I feel like Oscar knows me.

SHUMAN: I feel like I know you.

SAMANTHA: I feel like if you did, you wouldn't have thrown my mouse away!

SHUMAN: Your mouse?

SAMANTHA: Yes my mouse! I killed that!

SHUMAN: I know you killed it. It was going to start smelling so I threw it away.

SAMANTHA: It was mine.

SHUMAN: It was dead!

SAMANTHA: I loved that I killed that mouse and if you knew me at all you would have known that.

SHUMAN: How could I have possibly known that?

SAMANTHA: I told you.

SHUMAN: I feel like you didn't.

SAMANTHA: I feel like you weren't listening.

SHUMAN: I feel like you didn't try hard enough.

SAMANTHA: I feel like I did.

SHUMAN: Did you?

SAMANTHA: I did.

MATILDA: Did you?

SAMANTHA: Why are you taking his side?

MATILDA: I'm not taking anyone's side.

SAMANTHA: I feel like you're taking his side.

MATILDA: I feel like you're being resistant.

SAMANTHA: I feel like no one's listening to me.

MATILDA: I feel like you're not listening to yourself.

SHUMAN: I feel like I want to hold you Samantha.

SAMANTHA: I don't want you to.

SHUMAN: I feel like it's for your own good.

SAMANTHA: You don't know what's good for me. You don't know me.

SHUMAN: Let me know you.

SAMANTHA: You can't know me.

SHUMAN: I can if you let me.

MATILDA: He's right Samantha.

SAMANTHA: No he's not. He thinks I'm simple! I'm not simple! I'm complicated. He doesn't want to know that about me! He wants me to be simple! SIMPLE! SIMPLE! SIMPLE!!!!!

SHUMAN: I—I—I—I—

MATILDA: It's ok Shuman, let it out. Let it all out!

SAMANTHA: He's manipulating this! He's trying to—

SHUMAN: I love you Samantha. I love you!

MATILDA: Good Shuman. Good!

SAMANTHA: Don't coddle him. You wouldn't coddle me!

MATILDA: I'm not coddling him.

SHUMAN: I'm not being coddled.

MATILDA: I'm just trying to encourage him to express what he feels.

SHUMAN: No one coddles me.

SAMANTHA: No you coddle yourself.

SHUMAN: I do not. I—I—I—

SAMANTHA: There you go coddling yourself again!

SHUMAN: I'm not coddling myself. I'm starting to cry.

SAMANTHA: I feel like your crying isn't real. I feel like you're a fake. I feel like you have no backbone. I feel like you live in fear. I feel like you are a miserable lonely person.

SHUMAN: I feel like I don't know who you are.

SAMANTHA: I feel like that's what I've been trying to tell you.

SHUMAN: I feel disgusted by you.

SAMANTHA: I feel like I hate you.

SHUMAN: I hate you!

SAMANTHA: Then let me leave!

SHUMAN: Fine!

(SHUMAN starts to walk to the door. MATILDA gets up and rushes to the door, blocking SHUMAN's way.)

MATILDA: No!

SHUMAN:	SAMANTHA:
Get out of my way Matilda.	Get out of his way Matilda.

MATILDA: No.

SHUMAN & SAMANTHA: Yes!

MATILDA: You are not going to open that door Shuman.

SHUMAN: Yes I am.

MATILDA: I said no.

SHUMAN: But this is my house.

MATILDA: This is my session. And if I say you are not going to open this door. You are not going to open this door.

SHUMAN: I'll move you.

MATILDA: Try me. I know karate!

SHUMAN: I—I—I—I—

MATILDA: Shuman you will not let Samantha leave. That is not an option. Shuman you must stay strong. Tell me you are strong.

SHUMAN: I am strong.

MATILDA: Say it again and this time, mean it!

SHUMAN: I am strong!

MATILDA: Better. Again.

SHUMAN: I AM STRONG!!!!!

MATILDA: Good! GOOD!!! That's a breakthrough Shuman! Good! Here have a snack!

(*She throws him a snack. He catches it and eats it.*)

SAMANTHA: Why are you helping him Matilda? You don't even like Shuman!

MATILDA: I do like Shuman.

SAMANTHA & SHUMAN:	MATILDA:
You do?	I do?

MATILDA: I do.

SAMANTHA: Well if you like Shuman so much why don't you stay with him!

SHUMAN: What is she saying? I can't understand her. I just could but now I can't.

MATILDA: Samantha I told you before, it's because I care for you that I'm making you stay. Please, you're mixing the issues, you're—

SAMANTHA: You're making no sense.

MATILDA: What?

SAMANTHA: I said, that you're making no sense!

MATILDA: You want me to get you a glass of water?

SAMANTHA: No I don't want water. I want you to stop caring about Shuman!

MATILDA: I—did you just ask me to get you a plane ticket?

SHUMAN: Plane ticket? Where's she going?

MATILDA & SAMANTHA: SHHH!!!

SAMANTHA: Listen to me!

MATILDA: Samantha, I can't—I don't understand what you're saying. Are you alright?

SAMANTHA: No I'm not alright! I'm livid! STOP TAKING SHUMAN's SIDE!!!!!

MATILDA: A bologna sandwich? What?

SAMANTHA: UH!!! Will you listen to me? Please! I—

SHUMAN: What's she saying?

MATILDA: I don't know, I—I don't know.

SHUMAN: What do you mean you don't know?

MATILDA: I—I lost my connection, I—I—I can't understand her. I—Samantha? Are you hungry? Are you tired? Are you cold? Are you—uh—I don't know what to say. I'm failing! Oh god! I'm failing! Someone help me! I mean, I need to help you! I can help you. I think I can I think I can I think I can. I— *(She starts doing the Lamaze breathing.)* —I'm getting ahead of myself, my therapist tells me that's my fatal flaw, getting ahead of myself, but sometimes I just can't help it. Maybe I got ahead of myself by coming here today. I shouldn't have come. But you two need me! I know you do. And I know I was making progress, we just got derailed, we have to get back on track and then I can solve this and then I won't be so afraid to pursue my dream and I'll be a cat therapist full time and I won't have to work in that stupid vet's office or

moonlight at Hooters and I'll save cats everywhere
and I'll be fulfilled and loved. Sometimes though I
have a hard time believing anyone can ever love me.
Sometimes I think that I'm going to die alone and no
one will know me and I'll be found in a spider web of
my own macram and it'll take them four days to dig me
out of it— And I don't want to die that way! I CAN'T
DIE THAT WAY! OH GOD, I DON'T WANT TO DIE!
I WANT TO LIVE FOREVER! I WANT TO BE A
VAMPIRE! LIKE DRACULA! NO I DON'T! WHAT
AM I SAYING? WHAT'S HAPPENING TO ME?
I—I—I'm having a hard time breathing. Breathe
Matilda, BREATHE!!!!

(Just then there's a crash. OSCAR *falls into the room from the
ceiling. Everyone turns.)*

SAMANTHA: OSCAR?

OSCAR: SAMANTHA!

SAMANTHA: Oscar, how did you get—

OSCAR: I broke the skylight. I couldn't wait another
minute outside. I need to be with you. I need you with
me.

SAMANTHA: Oh Oscar! Take me! Take me away!

*(*OSCAR *starts to rush* SAMANTHA. SHUMAN *gets in the
way.)*

SHUMAN: Get away from her.

OSCAR: Don't tell me what to do.

SHUMAN: Get out of here! Get! NOW!!!

OSCAR: Not until Samantha leaves with me.

SHUMAN: Samantha is my cat!

SAMANTHA: You were just going to let me go!

SHUMAN: She stays here with me!

SAMANTHA: You can't do that.

SHUMAN: And she'll always stay here!

OSCAR: You're going to let us out of here buddy or else.

SHUMAN: Don't take another step, you hear me?

(OSCAR *takes another step.* SHUMAN *rushes in, picks up* OSCAR *and starts carrying him out.* OSCAR *is flailing.*)

OSCAR: No! NO! GET OFF ME!

(OSCAR *scratches* SHUMAN's *face.* SHUMAN *lets go of* OSCAR.)

SHUMAN: Ow! You—you—I—I—AH!!!!!

(SHUMAN *starts to chase after* OSCAR.)

SAMANTHA: Stay away from him! STAY AWAY FROM OSCAR!!!!

(SAMANTHA *starts to chase after* SHUMAN. *For a moment* MATILDA *can't quite decide whom to chase after. She then stops altogether.*)

MATILDA: Oh my. O K. (*She does more of the Lamaze breathing.*) O K and roll up and down your spine. Oh fuck it. ALRIGHT MOTHERFUCKERS EVERYBODY STOP!!!!!!!

(*Everybody stops.*)

MATILDA: Good. Ok. Now everybody find a seat.

(*No one moves.*)

MATILDA: FIND SEATS NOW!!!!

(*Everyone finds seats.*)

MATILDA: Good. Ok. (*She walks over to* OSCAR) Hello I'm Matilda you must be Oscar.

OSCAR: Aren't you a genius?

MATILDA: I'm not quite sure what you just said but I have no doubt that it was sassy. You may be an alley cat but while you're indoors you will behave with a modicum of respect. *Capiche*? I've always wanted to say that...so, *capiche*?

OSCAR: *Capiche.*

MATILDA: I think you just agreed, otherwise you said, fructose. Now. Clearly words aren't working for us. So I'm going to insist that we communicate for a while using physical gestures.

ALL THREE: Physical gestures?

MATILDA: Yes, something physical that tells how you feel. My therapist uses it all the time with me in my therapy. It's much simpler than words. Here, I'll demonstrate. I'm going to do a physical gesture and I want you all to tell me what I'm trying to say.

(MATILDA *stands up and does a bizarre and complex series of movements. She then turns to* SHUMAN, OSCAR *and* SAMANTHA.)

MATILDA: Well?

ALL THREE: Uh...

MATILDA: Think about it. It's really simple.

SHUMAN: You were trying to tell us that you were sad.

MATILDA: No. Samantha?

SAMANTHA: That you were hungry?

MATILDA: I didn't understand what you said but I'm certain it wasn't right. No. Oscar?

OSCAR: That you like orange groves?

MATILDA: No, I do not watch adult movies on Showtime!

OSCAR: That's not what I said! That's not what I—

MATILDA: Oh forget it! I was simply saying that I feel sometimes like a lonely hunter...looking for another meal...in a forest dense and dangerous...in a foreign country...that I've never been to before...in the heat of the summer solstice... Well, perhaps that wasn't so simple. But you get the gist, simply convey through a gesture, how you feel. I'm going to ask you all questions and I need you to answer them. O K?

(No answer)

MATILDA: O K??

ALL: Yes.

MATILDA: Show me with physical gestures!

(They all find various ways of saying "yes".)

MATILDA: Good. Now Samantha do you love Oscar?

SAMANTHA: Yes.

MATILDA: With a physical gesture. Again. Do you love Oscar?

(SAMANTHA *hugs herself tightly.)*

MATILDA: O K. Yes. O K, its obvious that Oscar loves Samantha, his breaking through the ceiling counting as his physical gesture. Now, Samantha do you love Shuman?

SAMANTHA: I don't know.

MATILDA: Physical gesture!

(SAMANTHA *does something to say, "I don't know.")*

MATILDA: O K, Samantha doesn't know if she loves you Shuman.

SHUMAN: Well I don't know if I love her either.

MATILDA: Are you sure or are you just saying that because she said it first.

SHUMAN: I don't know.

MATILDA: That's what I thought. *(Beat)* O K, so lets discuss compromises. Samantha if you could go outside, would you be willing to wear a leash and collar so Shuman could stay connected to you?

(SAMANTHA indicates the sensation of choking and dying.)

MATILDA: I'll take that for no. Shuman are you willing to let Oscar live inside with you?

(Both OSCAR and SHUMAN do gestures to indicate "Absolutely not".)

MATILDA: O K. Shuman are you willing to live outside with Oscar and Samantha?

SHUMAN: No!

MATILDA: Hmmm. Seems we've hit a sort of stumbling block. Give me a minute to strategize here.

OSCAR: *(Doing physical gestures while speaking)* I just gotta say... And I don't care who does or doesn't understand me. I don't want to compromise. I love Samantha and I want to be with her. I don't want to share her. I want her completely. And I'm willing to do anything for that. Anything.

(Beat. They all look at OSCAR. Everyone has understood him. Then, SHUMAN gets up.)

SHUMAN: Samantha, if you want to go. Go. I can't keep you.

MATILDA: No. *(She rushes to the door.)*

SHUMAN: Matilda, there's nothing left to do. She wants to go. I can't keep her.

MATILDA: But—no, I know if we fight through this, on the other side there's—

SHUMAN: But I don't want to fight through anything anymore.

SAMANTHA: Why should we have to fight? Shouldn't it be easy?

MATILDA: No, not all the time. It's not easy all the time.

SHUMAN: Matilda, move out of the way.

MATILDA: But—

SHUMAN: Matilda. Please.

(MATILDA *steps aside.*)

SAMANTHA *and* SHUMAN *stare at each other.*

SHUMAN: I, I just wish I were enough for you. But if I can't be, then I can't. Maybe I just held on to you too tightly.... (*He opens the door.*)

SAMANTHA: I just need to know.

SHUMAN: I know.

(*Beat. Then,* SAMANTHA *and* OSCAR *without looking back, run right out the door.* MATILDA *lingers in the doorway.*)

MATILDA: I—I feel so silly. (*She exits. The door shuts.*)

(*Quite suddenly we're outside. Everything changes. Light, sound, color, all are brighter, more vivid, more...wild.*)

(SAMANTHA *and* OSCAR *come running on.*)

SAMANTHA: We did it! You did it!

OSCAR: I did it! You did it!

BOTH: WE did it!

SAMANTHA: Wow! Will you look at it out here?

OSCAR: Yeah. Home sweet home!

SAMANTHA: It's so... wild!

OSCAR: So let me give you a quick tour....
This is fresh air.

SAMANTHA: *(Breathing in)* Hello air.

OSCAR: This is grass.

SAMANTHA: Hello grass.

OSCAR: And these are trees.

SAMANTHA: Hello trees.

OSCAR: And up there are clouds.

SAMANTHA: HELLO CLOUDS!!!!!!

OSCAR: And past the clouds is the sun.

SAMANTHA: HELLO SUN!!!!!

OSCAR: And down that way is a river.

SAMANTHA: Hello, river!

OSCAR: And I'm Oscar.

SAMANTHA: Hello Oscar.

OSCAR: Hello Samantha... And this is Oscar feeling shy.

SAMANTHA: Hi shy Oscar.

*(The stare at each other a moment, awkwardly...
and then...finally the two kiss.)*

SAMANTHA: I love you.

OSCAR: I love you too.

(He starts to lead her off.)

OSCAR: Come on.

SAMANTHA: Where are you taking me?

OSCAR: To the beach.

SAMANTHA: To the beach!!!!

(OSCAR *heads off in front of* SAMANTHA. *She starts to go and right before she's gone, turns to the audience.*)

SAMANTHA: So that's what we did. We headed to the beach. And along the way we stopped all over—in the big cities, deserts, mountains, you name it, Oscar and I saw it. And loved it. Every minute of it. Every detail.
   Think the Discovery Channel in 3-D.
   And then finally we made it to the beach. During the day there were tons of people around but at night, just like Oscar had promised, it was all ours.

(SAMANTHA *sits on the sand looking out.* OSCAR *enters.*)

SAMANTHA: Where were you?

OSCAR: I couldn't decide where to dump! There's so much sand!

(*Beat. The two stare out.*)

OSCAR: Isn't this heaven?

SAMANTHA: Yeah.

(*Beat*)

OSCAR: So I'm thinking that in a few days we should head out for Alaska. I hear its almost all snow there. Sound good?

SAMANTHA: Oh. Well I—

OSCAR: You what?

SAMANTHA: Nothing. I just thought—never mind.

OSCAR: No. Tell me. What?

SAMANTHA: I just thought we were going to stay here.

OSCAR: At the beach?

SAMANTHA: Yeah. I thought we were going to make this our home.

OSCAR: What do you mean?

SAMANTHA: I mean, I thought we'd make a house here.

OSCAR: Like with walls?

SAMANTHA: Yeah wouldn't that be fantastic?

OSCAR: It sounds kind of...small to me.

SAMANTHA: It wouldn't have to be... We could make it as big as we want.

OSCAR: But the whole world is our home. What's bigger than that?

SAMANTHA: Well I don't mean as big as the world, I just mean some place that's just ours. Our own place in the world.

OSCAR: I don't think I want a house. Look, Samantha, I'm an alley cat, I roam, that's all I've ever done.

SAMANTHA: We could try.

OSCAR: I don't think I could settle. I'm not sure it's in my nature.

SAMANTHA: We don't have to stay there all the time but wouldn't it be nice to have a place to go to...to know it's there?

OSCAR: I don't want that. I want to be free. I want to live on the sun and the sky and ground and our love.

SAMANTHA: I want our love to make a home.

OSCAR: Our love is home enough for me.

SAMANTHA: I don't think it's enough for me.

(Beat)

OSCAR: So.

SAMANTHA: So.

OSCAR: Where does that leave you and me?

SAMANTHA: Go to Alaska. Love Alaska!

OSCAR: But where will you be?

SAMANTHA: I don't know.

OSCAR: But how will I find you?

SAMANTHA: When you're ready, you just will. Oscar, I love you.

OSCAR: I love you too Samantha.

(The two kiss.)

OSCAR: See you soon sweetheart.

OSCAR *exits.*

SAMANTHA: *(To audience)* And then I was alone. For the first time in my life. I was alone. And for a while I didn't know what I was going to do. I knew I wanted a home. But I didn't know how to get one again.

And then one afternoon while passing through a city, I bumped into someone I never thought I'd see again.

(MOM enters. She looks fabulous. Very metropolitan. The two bump into each other.)

MOM: Oh excuse me.

SAMANTHA: It was my fault.

MOM: You look...familiar.

SAMANTHA: I think you're my Mom!

MOM: I think I am!

SAMANTHA: But what are you doing here? When I left, you were trapped in that house with those people?

MOM: Oh it's a tragic story. Really terrible. One afternoon, while everyone was out of town, the *faux* wood paneling mysteriously caught on fire and the house burned to the ground. Some say it was arson...

After that I made my way to the big city and started fresh.

SAMANTHA: That's great!

MOM: It is! And I'm now living with the most fabulous family who not only loves me immensely but also has impeccable taste. Think...Diane Keaton's house in "Something's Gotta Give". Do you live here too?

SAMANTHA: Oh...no, I was just passing through— I don't really—I'm a little lost I guess.

MOM: This is a very confusing part of the city. Are you going east or west?

SAMANTHA: No I mean, I'm lost. In my life. I don't know what I'm doing anymore.

(Beat)

MOM: You know, I was just going to get a soy milk, would you want to join me?

SAMANTHA: I think I would really like that. *(To audience)* And so I did. I spent the afternoon with my Mom drinking milk and talking about everything I'd been through. A few hours later, Mom turned to me and said—

MOM: I'm so proud of you Samantha.

SAMANTHA: For what? For messing everything up?

MOM: For living your life. For being you! For being Samantha. Samantha. That's a fabulous name by the way, did you name yourself?

SAMANTHA: No Shuman did. When he found me at the Shelter he named me.

MOM: You didn't tell me that before.

SAMANTHA: I—I guess I forgot.

MOM: That's a pretty big thing to forget.
  Would you look at the time? I should be getting back.

Every night the family does yoga together and it'd be strange if I wasn't there.

SAMANTHA: I understand.

MOM: This has been...fabulous.

(The two hug.)

MOM: Goodbye Samantha. *(She exits.)*

SAMANTHA: After Mom left all I could think about was Shuman and how much I wanted to see him. Just to see how he was.

And so I made my way back to Shuman's house.

And when I got there, I realized, I'd never really seen his house from the outside before. It's yellow. Isn't that funny! Shuman lives in a yellow house. And it looked so small, with the trees and mountains around it. So small and safe. And I couldn't help but go up to the window and peek in. Like so. *(She peeks in.)* And this is what I saw.

(SHUMAN *sits on the couch. He's crying.)*

SAMANTHA: I'd seen Shuman crying before. But somehow from the outside, looking in, he just seemed so vulnerable and beautiful and important to me. And everyday after that, I'd sneak up to Shuman's house and look through his windows and watch him.

I saw him cooking and singing and dancing and crying and sleeping and watching T V. And I saw him apologize to Matilda.

(MATILDA *and* SHUMAN *stand in the doorway.)*

SHUMAN: I'm sorry.

MATILDA: For what?

SHUMAN: For—Hey, do you want to, uh—

MATILDA: Sure.

(SHUMAN *lets* MATILDA *in.)*

SAMANTHA: *(To audience)* And from then on, Matilda always seemed to be around. And then one night, while the two sat on the couch, watching a sappy movie, Shuman turned to Matilda and said—

SHUMAN: Matilda, I,

MATILDA: Yes?

SHUMAN: I—

MATILDA: Yes?

SHUMAN: I...was thinking of ordering pizza for dinner. Do you want some?

MATILDA: Oh. Oh yes. Yes.

(The two stare at each other awkwardly.)

SAMANTHA: *(To audience)* And of course from the outside, it was so obvious that they were in love with each other. And as much as I wanted to be upset or hurt, all I could be was happy. Look at them. Look at the way they're looking at each other. Matilda loves Shuman unconditionally. And he loves her, unconditionally. And I realized in that moment that by letting me come outside, Shuman had told me that he loved me unconditionally too.

And I knew then that this was my home. I'd had it and I'd lost it and I wanted it back. And I didn't know if Shuman would let me back in but I decided that I had to try.

So that's what I did.

One evening, I just walked back to the house. When I got there, the door was shut. So I sat down and let out the loudest cry possible. Like so.

OPEN THE DOOR!!!!!!!!

*(*SHUMAN *and* MATILDA *hear* SAMANTHA *and run to the door and open it.)*

SHUMAN: Samantha?

MATILDA: Oh my!

SAMANTHA: *(To audience)*: And I looked Shuman right in the eyes and I said *(To* SHUMAN*)* Shuman, if you let me in, this is what I can promise you...

That I'll love you. Unconditionally.

I promise you I won't always understand you but I'll love you.

And sometimes I'll be confused by you but I'll love you.

And sometimes you won't get me and sometimes I won't get you but I'll love you.

And sometimes I may not know how to show it and sometimes I may not want to show it but I'll love you. And sometimes I may want to show it too much and you won't want to hear any of it and sometimes you'll want to show me and I won't want to see it but I'll love you.

And every once in a while, we'll be able to look into each other's eyes and for a moment, even if that's all it is, a moment, for that moment we'll understand each other and I'll love you then too.

And together we'll be free.

So...will you let me in?

(Beat)

SAMANTHA: *(To audience)* And for a second I wasn't sure if he understood everything I said or if he was going to close the door on me...but then...Shuman stepped out of the doorway...and let me in.

SAMANTHA: And I walked into my house, jumped onto the couch, curled myself into a ball and started to purr. *(She does all this as she says it.)*

SHUMAN: She's purring.

MATILDA: It means she's happy.

SHUMAN: I know.

SAMANTHA: *(To audience)* And I was finally home again. Home. And it was enough. And it has been. For all these years since then.

  Seventeen years to be precise. In this house. But Shuman and I haven't been alone. You see, right after I curled up on the couch, Matilda felt as though she should leave. So that's what she tried to do.

(MATILDA starts to leave.)

SHUMAN: Where are you going?

MATILDA: Oh my, well I thought I should go home and—

SHUMAN: Oh, well, uh, O K. I— O K.

MATILDA: O K. Then. O K.

SAMANTHA: *(To audience)* And I thought to myself that this is the most ridiculous thing I'd ever seen and that if after all they've done for me, I can't help them a little bit, well what's the point, so I did. I helped them. Like so.

(SAMANTHA quickly jumps off the couch and into MATILDA's arms.)

MATILDA: Oh my.

SHUMAN: I guess she wanted to say goodnight.

MATILDA: I guess. O K. Goodnight Samantha.

(She tries to get SAMANTHA off of her but can't.)

MATILDA: Oh my.

SAMANTHA: *(To audience)* I didn't let go.

MATILDA: She's dug her claws into my dress.

SHUMAN: Samantha. Let go.

SAMANTHA: No.

SHUMAN: SAMANTHA!

(SHUMAN *tries to get* SAMANTHA *off of* MATILDA. *He is attempting to pull her off and is pulling with much force.*)

SHUMAN: SAMANTHA*! LET GO!!!!!!*

SAMANTHA: O K. If you say so.

(SAMANTHA *lets go and then grabs onto* SHUMAN *who falls onto the floor.* MATILDA *falls on top of them.*)

MATILDA: Oh my.

SAMANTHA: *(To audience)* Worked like a charm. And then I just wriggled out of the way and let nature take its course.

MATILDA: Oh my. I already said that I think.

(Beat. The two look at each other. Then, finally—

SHUMAN: So, uh, I feel like I would like to kiss you now.

MATILDA: Oh, well, I feel like that would be a wonderful physical gesture.

SHUMAN: O K. O K. O K. Here goes. I'm going to kiss you now.

MATILDA: Oh my. O K... I think I should tell you that—

SHUMAN: Yes?

MATILDA: Well...I'm not simple Shuman.

SHUMAN: Me neither.

(*And with that* SHUMAN *grabs* MATILDA *and kisses her like a man kisses a woman in all your favorite romantic movies since the invention of film.*)

SAMANTHA: *(To audience)* And soon after that Shuman installed a new front door that had a flap in it, so I could come and go as I pleased. And I did. Like so. *(She goes through the door.)* Yeah, I'm outside! *(She goes back through the door.)* Yeah, I'm inside! *(To audience)*

And then soon after that Shuman built a website for Matilda's Cat Therapy Business and turned his extra bedroom into her office and soon she had more clients than she could ever have imagined.

(MATILDA *on the phone with a client.*)

MATILDA: Oh my. Well if Beverly wants to drink out of a wine glass let her. She's a grown cat, she knows what she wants. O K, let me know.

SAMANTHA: And soon after that, they got married. And then three years later, they had a baby boy. Named Abbott. And as Abbott got older he liked to chase me down the halls and try to pull my tail. Like so.

(ABBOTT *chases* SAMANTHA.)

ABBOTT: TAIL!!!!! LONG!!!!!

SAMANTHA: And I would bite him hard on the hand. Like so.

SAMANTHA *bites* ABBOTT *on the hand.*

ABBOTT: OW!!!!!! MOMMY!!!!!!!

SAMANTHA: But as we both got older, we found in each other a new friend. Like so.

ABBOTT: Sammy, you're so lucky you're a cat because you don't have to deal with stupid things like parents and school and girls. Is it possible to love a girl when you're only nine?

SAMANTHA: (*To audience*) And one night while I was roaming in the backyard, an old friend found me.

(OSCAR *appears.*)

OSCAR: Hey...sup sweetheart?

SAMANTHA: OSCAR!!!

(*The two run to each other and hug.*)

SAMANTHA: *(To audience)* And after that, whenever he was passing through, I'd spend the night outside with him.

(OSCAR and SAMANTHA lying outside together, looking at the stars.)

OSCAR: And then I met up with a pack of mountain cats and we climbed the Himalayas. Here, I brought you some soil from up there. Feels pretty much the same to me though.

SAMANTHA: *(To audience)* And time passed and life went on and things were good. Though that's not to say there weren't problems. Because there were, like the time Abbott got caught shoplifting.

MATILDA: Did you or didn't you pay for this?

ABBOTT: I don't know.

SHUMAN: Abbott! Answer your Mother!

ABBOTT: I didn't! I HATE YOU BOTH! *(He runs off.)*

SAMANTHA: *(To audience)* Or the time Matilda and Shuman had such a bad fight, Abbott and I hid under his blankets out of fear.

(We see ABBOTT and SAMANTHA huddled together under a blanket. Offstage we hear—)

SHUMAN: If I said we can't afford it, we can't afford it.

MATILDA: It doesn't seem like we can ever afford anything.

SHUMAN: Well if you could be a little more financially responsible Matilda, we could afford things.

MATILDA: Oh so it's my fault.

SHUMAN: It sure as hell isn't mine.

MATILDA: Don't talk to me like that. And don't you dare walk away from me.

SAMANTHA: *(To audience)* But whenever things got to be too much, Shuman would say—

SHUMAN: Everybody dance!

SAMANTHA: And we would. Like so.

(They all dance to something like Dexy Midnight Runner's Come on Eileen *together.)*

SAMANTHA: *(To audience)* And I got older. And older. And Oscar stopped coming. And I figured he'd probably died. And I hoped he was happy when he had and I let him go.

   And then about three days ago, I started to feel really... sick. Not like sick to my stomach but tired sick. Like my bones were tired and...I just knew.

   And so I've been waiting. And talking to you. Telling you about my life. For the first time, every detail.

(SHUMAN enters.)

SHUMAN: There you are. I've been looking all over for you. Are you O K?

SAMANTHA: No.

SHUMAN: Oh my sweet little baby. Oh, oh, oh, oh, oh....

(He picks SAMANTHA up.)

SHUMAN: I think we're going to have to take you to the vet. I'm so sorry I didn't find you earlier. I'm so sorry.

SAMANTHA: No. No vet. I'll be O K. I'll be fine.

SHUMAN: Shhh... They'll take care of you.

(SAMANTHA turns to SHUMAN and looks him in the eyes.)

SAMANTHA: Please Shuman, no vet. I don't want to die in the Vet.

SHUMAN: O K Sammy, no vet. Oh, I, oh, I. Then where do you want to be Samantha?

SAMANTHA: Right here. With my family.

SHUMAN: O K. Oh Sammy.

SAMANTHA: It's O K.

SHUMAN: Matilda! Abbott! Come here!

(MATILDA *and* ABBOTT *appear.*)

SHUMAN: I found Sam. She's—she doesn't want to go to the vet. She—

SAMANTHA: It's O K, you can say it.

SHUMAN: She wants to be here. In the house. With us.

MATILDA: Oh my.

ABBOTT: Oh Sam.

SAMANTHA: It's ok.

MATILDA: Samantha, you beautiful girl, you. O K.

(SHUMAN *rests her gently back on the floor and they all surround her. Beat—*)

ABBOTT: She's purring.

SHUMAN: Yes she is.

MATILDA: It means she's happy.

ABBOTT: Are you happy Samantha?

SAMANTHA: Yes. (*To audience*) I don't mean to be dramatic right now. Well, yes I do. But this would be a great time for some music. A great love song please.

(Silly Love Song *plays.*)

SAMANTHA: Thanks. That'll do. Here's exactly what I feel. I feel the rug under me. And under that I can feel the floor. And as I spread out further I can feel the ground, the soil, the earth, the world underneath me. And through the roof, I can feel the sun, hitting my coat like the warmest hands petting me. And I feel the faces of my family. Their eyes. And their hands on my body. And their love. Letting me go.

Maybe life is just this. Just this. This brief moment we have together where we're inside each other and outside ourselves and we can all just let go.

SHUMAN: Oh Samantha. I love you.

SAMANTHA: I love you.

MATILDA: I love you.

ABBOTT: I love you.

(*Lights fade.*)

END OF PLAY